-D(

PROMISES

TRUSTING GOD'S FAITHFULNESS

DEBBIE ADAMS

Divine PROMISES

BEYOND
PUBLISHING

New York | Los Angeles | London | Sydney

ISBN Hardcover: 978-1-63792-609-3
ISBN Softcover: 978-1-63792-597-3

TABLE OF CONTENTS

INTRODUCTION

Welcome to your wonderful journey into Divine Promises: Trusting God's Faithfulness. Enjoy a warm embrace as you discover the incredible power and unwavering love found in trusting God and His promises.

In a world that often feels chaotic and uncertain, it's comforting to know that we have a faithful and loving God who keeps His Word. The promises He has made are not empty or fleeting; they are steadfast and true. They offer us hope, guidance, and the assurance that we are never alone.

As you turn the pages of this book, you will encounter stories of my life experiences demonstrating how trusting in God's faithfulness will get you through this journey of life. These life experiences will hopefully inspire you and remind you that no matter what you're facing, there is always hope when you have God in your life. We will explore a wide range of divine promises, from finding peace in turmoil to experiencing abundant provision. From receiving healing to discovering the depth of His unconditional love, these promises will be like anchors for our souls.

This book is not just about gaining knowledge; it's about embracing a deeper relationship with God and allowing His promises to shape and transform our lives. It is written in hopes that you will open your heart to the beauty of His faithfulness and experience the peace and joy that comes from trusting God.

As you read this book, I invite you to embark on this journey with an open heart and anticipation to see what God will do in your life. Let's explore the divine promises and uncover the abundant blessings that await us when we put our trust in God's unwavering faithfulness.

CHAPTER 1

The Power Of Divine Promises

In God is my salvation and my glory: the rock of my strength,
and my refuge, is in God. Psalms 62:7

What is a Promise? What is a Divine Promise?

Webster defines a promise as "a declaration that one will do or refrain from doing something specified." It's also "a binding declaration that gives the person to whom it is made a right to expect or to claim the performance of a specified act." A promise is like a heart in that it's given out easily but also easily broken. A promise is meant to build trust between people, and when it's broken, the trust is broken.

Promises shouldn't be made if they're going to be broken; if you make a promise, you should keep it. How many times have we had someone tell us that they will help us and be there for us, but when the time comes, they can't be found and won't answer their phone? We've all heard the saying that hard times reveal who your true friends are – so anyone that truly keeps all their promises must be a true friend.

Of course, things do come up, and we're all human, so we sometimes fail in keeping promises, whether to our family or friends.

I'm sure we've all had someone in our lives make a promise and then let us down by not keeping it. But God never fails and will always keep His promises to us because God isn't human like us. Even though God created us, He's God and will not let us down. When God makes a promise, He will keep it.

Webster defines a divine promise as one that is "relating to or proceeding directly from God." A divine promise is a gift graciously bestowed, not a pledge secured by negotiation. These promises are the only kind of promises you can truly depend upon because they are from our all-mighty God.

There are many promises from God, but one that always comes to mind is the rainbow that we see in the sky. That is the promise from God that He won't send a flood to destroy the earth like He did with Noah and the ark. This is one of my favorite promises from God. "I do set my bow in the cloud, and it shall be for a token of a covenant between me and the earth" (Genesis 9:13). Every time I see a rainbow in the sky, I smile because I know that's God's promise to us that He won't destroy the earth again because of our sin.

Divine promises hold immeasurable power to shape our lives and draw us closer to God. Through belief and faith, we can unleash the potential of divine promises and experience a life filled with abundance, purpose, and fulfillment. Look at divine promises as our guiding light offering us hope, purpose, and direction. A purpose-driven life is a life of meaning.

I'm sure we've all had people ask us what our purposes in life are, or maybe you've spent some time questioning your own. God has a purpose and plan for each of us, so we need to pray daily and ask God for wisdom to see what His will is for our lives. "For I know the thoughts I think toward you, saith the Lord, thoughts of peace, and not of evil, to give you an expected end" (Jeremiah 29:11).

As we understand the reliability of the divine promises of God, we open ourselves up to a life filled with abundance, joy, and fulfillment. As you trust and have more faith in God, be prepared for all the blessings He will bestow on your life. Your life is a testimony for others to see, whether you realize it or not. People will be watching you when they see how God is changing your life. They will see that you have more peace and joy with Jesus, and they will see you smile a lot more.

I've always tried to be a happy person no matter what is going on in my life. I admit there have been times that I had to seek out a reason to smile, and it always came back to Jesus. He will always give you a reason to smile. People have asked me through the years why I'm always smiling, and my response is always that it's better than frowning. Then I tell them that Jesus is my reason for smiling because no matter what, I know that He is always with me.

A lot of times it's not what we say to others but what our life says to others. If you're anything like me, you're a people watcher. I love watching people, and I really love watching how God is changing people's lives for the better. There is always a reason to be happy and thankful. Take time to remind yourself what you are thankful for. I'm thankful every day for all the many ways God has and still is blessing my life. I'm always thankful for God saving my soul from Hell and keeping me healthy. Let's follow God's guiding light and see where it will take us.

The nature of divine promises is characterized by their unwavering certainty and reliability. You will find that God is very reliable, if you don't know already. In fact, He is the only reliable source you need because people are not that reliable. God's promises act as beacons of hope, illuminating the path through life's uncertainties. How do we conquer all of life's challenges without God's help? There isn't a way that I've found to make it through life and all its challenges without God. God is my everything, and I depend on Him every day.

Divine promises offer comfort in times of hardship, reminding us that we are not alone in this journey called life. Through belief, the transformative power of these promises becomes accessible, empowering us to navigate life's challenges with courage. Faith, hope, and purpose will guide us toward a life enriched by the power of God. Divine promises provide assurance and support in our lives. They provide a foundation of faith and hope, offering guidance in navigating life's complexities and finding spiritual fulfillment.

No matter what we face in life, God is always with us, according to His promises. We are never alone. I hope you're beginning to see how God's promises are better than ordinary promises. The promises of God are priceless, and they are our assurances of His love and faithfulness toward us.

Do you have something that you consider priceless in your life? Maybe you have a family heirloom or comforting item that you think you would be lost without. Well, God is like that to me, and He can be that to you as well. God is eternally faithful and true to us and will be forever. God loves us, and He gave us all these promises to show us how much. All we need to do to receive these promises is to pray to God and believe that He will fulfill them.

I've heard people say, "Oh, I prayed, and nothing happened." To that, I will ask, how much faith did you have, and are you truly believing in God? We must first believe that what we're asking for will come into being. Sometimes God will make us wait on things until we start believing that He will do what He promises. I've been in that situation before, where I know God will perform a miracle in my life, and I do believe, yet there are still doubts. Often, Satan will keep us doubting. I'm not perfect; none of us are. However, I've learned a lot over the years about believing and receiving, and God's Word is true.

These promises come from our Almighty God, who is Infinite and cannot lie. He will always take care of us. We can have faith that God, in His time, will fulfill his divine promises to bring us great blessings.

These promises rest upon several things which make them true, just like a house must rest upon a good foundation to stand. One such tenet is God's Holiness, as God is Holy, and He cannot deceive. "For the Mighty One has done great things for me; and Holy is His name" (Luke 1:49). God's promises are also supported by his goodness. He is a good God, which means He will not forget. God's truth is another element because God will not change, and He is the same yesterday, today, and tomorrow. Finally, God's power accomplishes and fulfills these promises in our lives.

Divine promises, as I see them, are God giving us His heart and letting us see how much He truly loves us. Through these promises, God reveals His mind and will to us. These promises are dear and precious to the heart of God, and they will become precious to us in all the many ways that He delivers them.

Thinking back over the years and seeing how God kept His promises to me, I can smile knowing He was there taking care of me in every situation. Instead of being surprised that He could fulfill His promises, we must simply thank Him for helping us. These promises are God's free gifts of favor to us, so welcome them and trust in them.

Throughout the Bible, God is seen as the promise maker, and He will always keep His Word. We can obtain every promise of God if we reach out and claim what the Lord Jesus has given us. God's Word applies to every area of our lives, and He has given us promises for everything that we will go through in our lifetime. We need to glorify what God has done for us so we can be witnesses to others regarding how faithful God is and will be through His promises.

A promise from God is a declaration of expectation that we know we will receive. God will not fail to keep His promise because

He is a righteous God, and His character is righteous. There are many people in our lives we consider to have good character, but God, in his righteousness, has the best character of all.

God has given us promises in His Word, and He will fulfill them for us, but we need to remember it will be in His timing and not ours. God's timing isn't always with our timing. Our human nature drives us to want things done instantaneously, but God has a different timespan. He knows the perfect time to fulfill His promises to us. We should let God become bigger than our problems, and then our problems won't seem so huge. Only then will everything fall into place. We need to see that God has a reason for everything that happens in our lives. Learn to stand on God's promises no matter what circumstances come into your life. When you say you have faith in God, what you are saying is that you have faith in God's promises and what He has promised to fulfill.

People without hope in God or His promises do not have peace in their lives. Their minds and hearts rely on their own strength and not God's, so they will not have rest and peace. "And the peace of God, which passeth all understanding, shall keep your hearts and minds through Christ Jesus" (Philippians 4:7).

When we rest on the promises of God, there is peace that passes all understanding. God is faithful, good, and able to deliver His promises according to His will. So, let's explore the promises God has for us in this journey of life.

CHAPTER 2

PROMISE OF REDEMPTION:

Restoring Brokenness

Trust in the Lord with all thine heart; and lean not unto thine own understanding. In all thy ways acknowledge Him, and He shall direct thy paths. Proverbs 3:5-6

What comes to your mind when you think about redemption? Webster defines redemption as "to free from what distresses or harms." There are many promises from God about redemption and restoration. How many times have we gone through something and wondered how it could ever be fixed or how life would ever be the same? We might even try to fix things on our own before taking them to God, when God should be our first source of help. Believe me, I've tried to fix many things before, and when I finally gave up and let God take over, everything turned out so much better. God's power through His promise of redemption will restore brokenness, heal hearts, and breathe new life into our existence, even if we thought there was no chance of repair.

I'm sure you have heard the saying that you're either in the valley or on the mountaintop. There was a time in my life that I wondered what was going to happen next because, for about a two-year span, it seemed I stayed in the valley. Something seemed to always be happening. Our Preacher always said that you're either going through a storm, you just came out of a storm, or one is headed your way, and that storm lasted for two years of my life. It wasn't that I was doing something wrong; I was in church all the time, helping out and singing in the choir, and I was reading my Bible and praying to God daily. Just because you're going through a storm or some situation in your life doesn't necessarily mean that God is punishing you because we're tested throughout our lives.

Sometimes God will even use us and what we're going through to speak to others by showing them our faith. I do believe that God was using me to speak to someone else by showing them that my faith was in God and not in myself. Obedience is a key part of God's testing because sometimes He will test our faith in Him. "Because you know that the testing of your faith produces perseverance" (James 1:3).

I've always been the cheerful, happy person who always had a smile; however, during the long storm in my life, I felt as though my life was upside down at times. However, through it all, God changed me for the better.

It all started when I got cancer, and my husband left me. I had always been healthy, and suddenly, out of the blue, I got cancer. When the doctors told me the news, I felt like someone had stabbed me in the heart. Anyone that has had cancer knows what I'm talking about. God knew it was going to happen even before it happened because it was in His plan. At the end of my cancer treatments, my husband decided to end our marriage, and it was like a truck had run over my heart. I felt like it had shattered into a million pieces.

I kept my trust in God even though I was having a hard time finding a reason to smile. My life had always been easy; there had been no major problems at all until this point, so I was very unsure of what to expect next. Through this, I learned that God will always help you with whatever you're going through, and even when you think you can't handle it, be assured that God can and will. The one thing I did know was that God was on my side no matter who else was or wasn't. I had to lean on God and trust Him, for my life depended on it. If you can't trust God, who can you trust? I knew I would get through this storm with God's help, and He held my hand the whole way.

Looking back now, 14 years later, I'm thankful for God's promises. "I will never leave thee nor forsake thee" (Hebrews 13:5). God never left me; I felt His presence very clearly in my life.

You might remember the poem "Footprints in the Sand." Well, the last verse in that poem says, "When you saw only one set of footprints, it was then that I carried you." I believe the Lord carried me a lot in those two years of trials. If it hadn't been for my Lord, I know I wouldn't have made it. God loves us and wants to help us. All we have to do is to call out to Him, and He will be there.

Redemption symbolizes the opportunity for a fresh start, forgiveness, and transformation. It is a journey that has the potential for healing and growth. Redemption is a light shining in the darkness, a flicker of hope whispering restoration to mend that which has been shattered. Believe me, I did feel at times like my life was shattered but I also knew God would put all the pieces back together and make it something even more beautiful – and He did. It was as if my life was a puzzle, and God was putting all the pieces together to create something amazing and brand-new. Looking back on that time, I smile and see how God made my life even more beautiful.

Redemption isn't solely about repairing what's broken but transforming it into something new. Have you ever gotten an old piece of furniture that someone threw out and thought you could repaint it and make it look new again? That's exactly what God does for us in His redemption promise. He takes us in whatever shape we're in and makes us more beautiful than before. Let your test become your testimony. Nothing is too hard for God; whatever we're going through, He can refine it like precious gold and make it sparkle beautifully. Redemption is our testament to how God promises to transform us into something new so we can rise above our past into something new, showing love, compassion, and understanding to others.

I can now look in the rearview mirror and see how far I've come and how far God has taken me. Today, life is good. God is good. God gave me a new husband almost 11 years ago. I saw God's hand in putting us together, and I'm so thankful for my abundant blessings from God.

Redemption can offer comfort to those burdened by guilt or haunted by past mistakes. Through the promise of redemption, God helps us rebuild, reconcile, and reclaim our true selves. When I was going through my dark valley, I had lost my true self, and through God's power of mercy and grace and His promise of redemption, I was able to find myself again. I rediscovered the joy and happiness I once had, and I was smiling again. It will be a journey that requires courage, forgiveness, and self-reflection, but the outcome will be renewed purpose, inner peace, and the chance to create a better future. Isn't it amazing what God will do for us if we just let Him? The promise of redemption allows us to transcend the scars of the past into the transformative power of second chances. God always promises us second chances.

What are you struggling with that you need to let God take care of for you? God is willing and able to help you with anything; it doesn't matter what it is because God already knows all about it. Whatever you're fretting about remember God's promise of redemption. Let God take over your life and see what His guiding light will do for you. Trust me, it will be incredible.

God's promise of redemption is a profound testament to His boundless love and mercy, which he shows to us every day. Although we will face trials and struggles while we're in this world, God's promise of redemption is unshakeable. In times of despair, we can know that

God's redemptive plan is at work, bringing healing, renewal, and eternal joy to all those that put their trust in Him.

We live in a world full of hardship, and sometimes it can feel like there is no hope for tomorrow. No matter how broken you may feel, God can still restore you. God's love toward us is unconditional; He doesn't look at our past mistakes and failures like we do because He wants to heal our brokenness and show us His mercy and grace. He loves to see the smiles on our faces and our energy after we're restored to living our life to the fullest. We don't deserve God's mercy or grace, yet He loves us so much, He wants to give it to us anyway.

When we focus on God's promises and His faithfulness, we can find strength and hope for each day. Through prayer and surrender, we ask God to restore our lives to something beautiful, as only he can do. "My grace is sufficient for you, for my power is made perfect in weakness" (2 Corinthians 12:9).

I could not have imagined how God would bring me out of my brokenness, yet He did, and so amazingly that all I could do was smile and be thankful. Our brokenness has the power to bring new beauty, strength, and inspiration to others. God is our restorer and healer, and He doesn't just patch us up; He mends and repairs us and creates an even better work of art in us. Our life is like a puzzle that God puts together piece by piece, even when He must mend it or even create new puzzle pieces.

God's promise of redemption isn't only forgiveness of sins but also the restoration of a relationship with God and the hopes of eternal life. We should repent, seek forgiveness, and seek God's transformative power in our lives. God's redemptive power can heal and restore what's broken, whether it's broken relationships, broken hearts, or broken lives. God's love and grace has the power to bring wholeness and healing to our brokenness whether it's due to sin in our lives, suffering, or consequences of our actions.

Since we are flawed and sinful, we're separated from a perfect and Holy God. This is why we have brokenness, suffering, and a need for redemption. God's promise of redemption comes from His desire to reconcile with humanity is an expression of His unconditional love and grace toward us. God's transformative power gives us spiritual growth, personal renewal, and a new way of life.

Redemption through restoration is a process where we are continually conformed to the image of Christ. Some days, we succeed at being who God wants us to be, and other days, we need God's transformative power in our lives. God will extend His mercy and grace continually so that we may work toward becoming Christ-like. The promise of redemption also includes the hope of eternal life because we can have a restored relationship with God both in this world and in Heaven. This promise provides comfort, purpose, and the assurance of a future beyond our life on this earth. God's promise of redemption is also linked to God giving His only son Jesus, who willingly offered Himself as a sacrifice, to atone for the sins of humanity. This provided a way for us to be forgiven and reconciled with God.

Redemption involves the restoration of our honor, dignity, or spiritual well-being after experiencing sin, guilt, or wrongdoing. Redemption is associated with seeking forgiveness, making amends, and transforming our lives. It can be a deeply personal and transformative journey involving recognition of wrong, atonement, growth, forgiveness, and healing. Whatever we go through in our lives, our transformation to something new and beautiful will give us an amazing new purpose in life.

CHAPTER 3

PROMISE OF PROVISION:

Meeting Every Need

*But my God shall supply all your need according to His
riches in glory by Christ Jesus. Philippians 4:19*

We've talked about the promise of redemption, and now we're
going to talk about the promise of provision and how God meets
every need. Provision simply means providing for and/or meeting
a specified need. From the necessities of food, shelter, and clothing
to the fulfillment of our dreams, we often find ourselves in need of
various things. Whatever need you have, take it to God, and He will
meet it.

I remember a time several years ago when I had gotten a new
job after being out of work for a while, and a gentleman at church gave
me an envelope and told me he wanted to help me because it would be
a couple of weeks before I got paid. I didn't open the envelope until I
got home, but it was a lot of money. God was taking care of a need He
knew I would have without me even asking. At the end of the year, I

gave the gentleman back his money and I was so thankful that it was there when I needed it and that I was able to pay him back.

God always takes care of His children and always keeps His promises. God will take care of all your needs, whether physical, emotional, financial, or spiritual. God's promise of provision once again reminds us that we're not alone in our journey of life. However, we must remember that this promise doesn't guarantee that every want and desire will be fulfilled. It doesn't mean that you will have a life free of challenges or hardships. It simply means that the fundamental aspects of life will be provided for. By focusing on God's blessings already in our lives, we can have a deeper appreciation for the resources and opportunities that come our way. You might think that provision is about possessions or financial gain, but it's more than that. It also includes love, support, and guidance. Everyone's journey in life is different, and God meets and provides for our needs according to our specific life circumstances.

Maybe you have a need for love, but you're all alone. Perhaps God will put you in a position to help others, and by showing them love, you, in turn, will receive the love you were seeking. You might need support and guidance with something going on in your life, and God will put someone in your path to help you. I hope you're beginning to understand that God is a loving, reliable, and faithful God, and we can depend on Him to keep the promises He gave us in His Word. Just pray and ask Him for what you need, and He will supply it. God already knows what you need because He's all knowing; however, He wants to hear directly from you.

Ask, and you shall receive; knock, and it shall be opened to you; seek, and you shall find. These are simple promises that God gives us every day. Do you need gas in your car or food but don't have the money, and then a check comes in the mail? Well, that was not a coincidence, it was God. Who do you think knew that you wouldn't have enough money? He had already put things in motion so you would get the check in the mail at just the right time. God loves you and will always take care of your needs.

"And all things whatsoever ye shall ask in prayer, believing, ye shall receive" (Matthew 21:22). Whenever you pray to ask God for a need or a want, you need to believe that God will fulfill it. God already knows our hearts, so He knows whether you believe when you ask. When we have faith, we will be richly blessed by God. I'm not saying God won't answer your prayers, but He might make you wait until your faith is stronger. I've had to wait for some things, and other times, I've gotten prayers answered right away. When I had to wait, it was because I was like the "oh ye of little faith" that God talks about in His Word. God was waiting until the right time – when my faith was stronger, and I was ready. Through faith and trust, we can find solace in knowing that our needs will be fulfilled by our loving God.

We are meant to depend on God for our provisions. We should look to Him to provide for us when our own means seem inadequate.

Think about God feeding the 5,000 in the Bible. That's a good example of God providing when other means are inadequate. God will always provide for your needs. Your wants can always wait, yet sometimes God provides those too. If you want a Lamborghini, that is an extravagant want – so you might need to do some serious praying about that.

When you put your trust in God, He will protect, provide, and care for you, although sometimes it's not in the way you might expect. He gives us what He knows we need and not necessarily what we want. If God knows that giving you something you want will harm you in some way, then as your Heavenly Father, He might not give it to you. Alternatively, he might wait until the time is right. He might be waiting for you to grow and mature before giving you a want.

I remember a few times when I was looking for a new job, either because I had gotten laid off or simply wanted a better one, but it didn't come immediately. I kept praying and wondering why God wouldn't allow me to obtain a job. He was either protecting me, His child, or waiting for my growth so I would be ready for it. There were jobs I had applied or even interviewed for only to later hear something bad about them. I saw then that the Lord was protecting me from a bad environment. It's no different than if your four-year-old wants a motorbike. You might not get it for them, because you know that they're too young and they could get hurt. You might tell them that they can get it when they're older. The Lord knows the future, unlike us, and He knows what will harm us. So, we might not always get our wants, but God will always provide for our needs.

God's promise of provision is seen in the context of a trusting relationship with Him. There are several instances in the Bible where God shows His promise of provision by meeting people's needs. In Matthew 6:25-34, Jesus encourages His followers not to worry about their material needs because God knows about them and will provide. You don't need to worry about your needs because God will always provide.

Remember in the Bible when the widow woman and her son only had enough flour and oil to make one cake of bread, and then they were going to die? Well, God provided for her needs. God sent His prophet Elijah to them, and he asked her to make him a little cake before making one for herself and her son. She did what he asked and made him a little cake of bread, and then God provided her enough flour and oil so she could eat, and her barrel never ran dry. "For thus saith the Lord God of Israel, the barrel of meal shall not waste, neither shall the cruise of oil fail, until the day that the Lord sendeth rain upon the earth" (I Kings 17:14).

If God can provide food for a widow woman and her son so they don't need to worry about having enough to eat, think about what God is able to do for you and me and our needs. He might not send a prophet to us; however, He will provide in some way, perhaps by sending someone to us or giving us money in the mail. When I was on unemployment and looking for a job, God opened the right door for me, and I got a job offer on the day of my last unemployment check. It was a great job, and years later, God moved me to an even better job where I can work from home and be with my husband, cat, and family. It's the job of my dreams, and I love it. I'm so thankful that God opened the door and gave it to me.

I could see God's hand in every aspect of my job, from the interview to the job offer. God is always on time – and right on time – in every situation. Take your needs to God, and He will take care of whatever it is as He promises. His promise of Provision is true, and He will meet every need you have because He already knows what you need before you even ask.

God's promise of provision shows us that God is a loving and caring Heavenly Father who will always provide the needs of His children. As we've talked about previously, people might not always do what they promise, but you can always trust that God will faithfully deliver your needs and always answer your prayers. It might not always be the answer you were looking for, but I promise you, it will be even better. God has never failed in any of His promises to me my entire life, and I know without a doubt that He never will. While our needs change and vary between different people, God will never change, and His provision for our needs is constant and sufficient. God is all we need every day.

Sometimes, our needs are not material but spiritual, and God will tend to those as well. As humans, we notice when we need basic items like food or water, but only God knows what spiritual needs you have and how to supply them. We all need to keep a check on our spiritual needs and strive to be closer to God by reading His Word and praying daily. This world sometimes seems to get in the way of our connection with God, especially now with all the electronics and social media. It might be wise to make time to shut out the world and talk to God about your basic needs as well as your spiritual needs. I know I've had to do that before. Don't wait to call on God until something major happens in your life and you need Him to help with an emergency. Call on Him daily. God is our provider, and he will deliver.

Ultimately, this promise of provision encompasses both emotional and spiritual needs as well as basic needs of food, shelter, and finances. It also includes comfort, guidance, peace, and strength during difficult times. God's promise of provision is about meeting all the needs of a person. God cares about the whole person and everything they need to live a complete life.

The fulfillment of God's provision is seen in His faithfulness, timing, and the ways He works in our individual lives. God's fulfillment at times can be seen as miraculous, such as when He gave me a job just as my unemployment was running out. God is a miracle worker; I've seen Him perform many miracles in my own life as well as those of my family and friends.

Don't ever think that God doesn't care about you and your needs because He does. If you aren't living right or are doing something that others look down on, you might think that God isn't there and doesn't care. My friend, He does care, and He is there helping you even when you don't notice. God has angels on this earth helping take care of us too. Do you ever wonder why the car you saw run the red light didn't crash into your car, instead barely missing you? Well, that was God taking care of you and His angels ever so gently standing in the way so your car wouldn't be hit. After all, you don't have the money for a car repair bill, and God knows it. God takes care of us in unseen ways that we don't realize. If you think about all the little ways in life you're blessed by God, it's simply amazing.

I hope you see that this promise of provision includes everything you could ever need. God will provide for us through employment opportunities, as He has for me in the past, unexpected provisions, such as a check in the mail for a much-needed bill, or the support of other people. God has put people in my path to guide me and help me with my needs many times. As you can see, God has a variety of different ways to provide for us. Matthew 6:26-27 says, "Behold the fowls of the air: for they sow not, neither do they reap, nor gather into barns, and yet your Heavenly Father feedeth them. Are you not much better than they? Which of you by taking thought can add one cubit unto his stature?" If God will take care of the birds, which are considered lesser in value, think about how much more He will take care of you and me.

CHAPTER 4

PROMISE OF PROTECTION:

Finding Security In God

God is our refuge and strength, a very present help in trouble.

Psalm 46:1

There may be times when you need God's protection in one way or another. Protection simply means "to cover or shield from exposure, injury, damage, or destruction," according to Webster. God is always there to take care of us with whatever our needs might be, and the need for protection isn't any different from the other promises. Finding security and solace and seeking the protection of God is a deeply personal and meaningful journey. It can provide a sense of comfort, guidance, and assurance during challenging times. Believing in the promise of divine protection can offer a source of strength and hope, helping us navigate through life's uncertainties.

A few years ago, during a storm, we received a tornado warning. I gathered my dogs and cat and went into the biggest closet in the house. I had never been close to a tornado at all, and I was home alone, as my husband had taken my car to get an oil change. I wasn't sure what to do, but I did know we needed to take shelter. As I sat in the closet with my animals and observed the looks of fright on their faces, I began praying that the storm would pass over us. I held onto my Bible while listening to the tornado warnings on my radio, and I knew we would all be ok. Like the song says, "Precious Lord, hear my cry. Keep me safe till the storm passes by." That is exactly what happened. God kept His promise and protected us from the storm.

My neighbor said he saw the tornado on top of our house, and then it just moved and left. He was brave enough to be outside on his patio watching it, but not me. I heard it over the house because it sounded very loud, like a train. When I heard what my neighbor said, I knew that it was the hand of God protecting us.

God will protect you from a tornado storm as well as other kinds of storms in your life. A sense of security is formed knowing that God offers shelter and security to those that seek refuge in Him. In times of uncertainty, the promise of protection offers a beacon of hope. This promise provides a sense of peace gained from knowing that God is steadfast and unmovable, guarding and shielding his children from harm.

Embracing the promise of protection involves trust and faith in God. We talked about this in the previous chapter, and it applies to all of God's promises. If you don't have trust and faith in God, then you won't believe that His promises are true and that He will keep them. We need to cultivate a deep relationship with God, seeking His guidance and surrendering to His will. To do this, we need to pray, meditate, fast, and study the Bible. The promise of protection offers the assurance that during difficulties, God walks with us, providing strength, wisdom, and comfort. It is that sense of strength and hope that can help us through life's trials.

I'm sure we all remember the year 2020 and the fear that people had because of the so-called pandemic. Well, God was taking care of us through that too. A lot of people were fearful that Covid-19 would make them extremely or fatally ill. I wasn't fearful because I was trusting God, but I must admit, I was a little concerned. God tells us that He "…has not given us the spirit of fear; but of power, and of love, and of a sound mind" (2 Timothy 1:6-7). How many people do you know that three years later, are still fearful, won't go out anywhere without a mask, and will take any shot you offer them?

I'm not saying that Covid isn't real, because it is real, and I lost several family members to it. I even got a mild version of it in 2022, which seemed like the flu. During that whole time, I prayed for God's protection and asked Him to keep it out of our house, and He did. My point is that we should trust God to take care of us and protect us, and He will. When we're being fearful and worrying, we giving into what Satan wants. Satan loves it when we don't fully trust God because it means he's getting us to doubt. Don't think that I've never been fearful or worried because I have; however, God brought me back to reality, and then I started fully trusting God again.

When we put our trust and faith in God, we can see that He will be our refuge and fortress and a protector from harm and danger. We can then experience peace and assurance knowing that God is watching over us. After all, God gives us a peace that passes all understanding. If you've never experienced this peace, then you might not know what I'm talking about, but when you have the peace of God in your heart, it's a peace like no other. During moments when I might be concerned or troubled about something, I can sense God's presence in the room with me and around me. That's the peace I need in those moments.

God's promise of protection doesn't necessarily mean a life free of hardships or adversity because since we still live on Earth, there will always be something to deal with. We're just passing through Earth on our way to Heaven, and while we're here, we need God every minute and every hour of every day to help us face our challenges. God will always be there for us, as He promised to help us navigate difficult times and take care of not only our physical safety but also our emotional, mental, and spiritual well-being.

I used to take the bus to work instead of driving an hour in busy traffic, so I had to walk a block after I got off the bus. At first it was a little nerve-racking because I had never had to walk to get to work before, but God gave me the peace of mind that He would take care of me. There was also a time years later that I had to fly to California by myself, which involved figuring out the airport alone to make sure I arrived where I needed to go. That time, I felt the peace of God the whole time, and I wasn't nervous at all. That trip marked the beginning of becoming an author, as it was when I attended a book writing retreat. I also met up with a friend of mine for some

California adventures. No matter what you're facing in life, God will give you peace and protect you. "And the peace of God, which passeth all understanding, shall keep your hearts and minds through Christ Jesus" (Philippians 4:7).

God serves as our source of refuge and strength, offering assistance and protection in times of distress. After all, we are His creation – and he wants to take care of His creation to make sure we're protected and safe. "..... Lo, I am with you always, even to the end of the world" (Matthew 28:20).

God's promise of protection should make us feel thankful that we have a loving Heavenly Father who loves to take care of us. The kindness that God shows us and the protection He provides is nothing but grace. He is full of mercy and grace towards us, His children. In times of difficulty or fear, we can have hope knowing that God's protective hand is on us. How many times have we taken road trips and prayed for God's protection to be on us and our car? We know that God is the only one that can truly protect us should any harm try to come our way.

You might be wondering about all the disasters and deaths in the world and why they occur if God is protecting us all. Well, God is still offering protection during those disasters. He has plans for each of our lives. It might not look like protection when people die, but God might be removing them from this earth to protect them from the bad things happening. After all, God is the only one that can see and know the future.

Let's talk about Job. I'm sure you all remember that Bible story. How did God protect him if he lost everything except his life? What happened to Job was because of Satan. Satan thought Job would turn against God, so Satan asked God if he could test him. God did protect Job in that Satan wasn't allowed to kill him in his trials. Job showed how strong his faith was, even though I'm sure he might not have understood why he was going through so many hardships. He lost his family and friends, his money, and his health. Even Job's wife told him to curse God and die, but he kept his faith in God because he knew God would take care of him no matter what. As a result, Satan failed, and God blessed Job abundantly, restoring everything he lost. We all need to keep our faith strong like Job, no matter what life brings our way. I do know that it gets very hard sometimes to hold on to your faith, but we all need to stay strong. Sometimes, we just need to let "Jesus take the wheel," as the song says, and get out of His way, so He can work out His plans for our lives.

God protects us from unseen dangers that come into our lives. God's protection doesn't exclude the possibility of harm or death, but be assured that whatever you go through, God is still taking care of you and protecting you. God will always provide protection from temptations of sin, which threaten to take us off course from where we need to be. "Because thou has made the Lord, which is my refuge, even the most High, thy habitation; there shall no evil befall thee, neither shall any plaque come nigh thy dwelling" (Psalm 91:9-10). With God on our side, our enemies don't have a chance.

Job's story shows us that God's promise of protection doesn't prevent us from pain or loss. Sometimes it might not be His will to deliver us out of something, but through it all, God will protect you. Sometimes the trials we go through are how God purifies us. By allowing trials in our lives, God tests our faith and, in the end, makes it stronger, so that we can persevere and grow more mature. In the end, you will be totally blessed.

God promises to also protect us from the evil of the world. "The Lord shall preserve thee from all evil; He shall preserve thy soul. The Lord shall preserve thy going out and thy coming in from this time forth, and even for evermore" (Psalms 121:7-8). In times of trouble, you can find refuge in God's protection. God is our protector, and His Word gives us comfort, hope, and strength in times of need.

God is all-knowing, all-powerful, and compassionate. He watches over us and offers guidance and protection daily. The protection from God isn't only for avoiding from harm but also for providing guidance and direction in our lives. God can also intervene on our behalf, offering unexpected solutions to what we thought were impossible situations. So, the promise of protection gives us a sense of purpose and brings us comfort and strength, knowing that we're not alone. God will give us inner peace during moments of distress when we may be going through trials and testing. Whenever you're going through something, turn it over to God and have faith and believe that He will protect you.

CHAPTER 5

PROMISE OF GUIDANCE:

Navigating Life's Path

Thy word is a lamp unto my feet, and a light unto my path.
Psalms 119:105

What does guidance mean to you? Guidance is directing or leading someone through a problem or an issue with help and/or advice. How many times have you wanted to do something you know nothing about, and a friend gives you insight on how to accomplish it? Perhaps you had an issue you were trying to resolve, and someone gave you advice about what to do. These are instances of guidance. God also gives us guidance in our daily lives.

God has a plan and a specific will for each of us, and He will guide us to follow His will. You might think that you're going about life doing what you want; however, God is guiding and directing your life. Only God knows if something will be bad for you, so He will direct you away from it. Yes, there are times when we don't listen to God. In these circumstances, Satan is trying to take over by making us think something is good when it's not. Later, you realize that you should have prayed about it and listened to God instead. "And thine ears shall hear a word behind thee, saying, this is the way, walk ye in it, when ye turn to the right hand, and when ye turn to the left" (Isaiah 30:21).

Through His promise of guidance, God offers us a great source of comfort and assurance, knowing that we're not alone and that God is always there to help guide us in any situation. God has been my guiding force for many years and through many of life's situations. In God's infinite wisdom and compassion, He offers guidance to those who sincerely seek it. This promise of guidance shows us that through prayer and seeking God's guidance, we will be provided with the wisdom, clarity, and direction we need on our journey of life.

There have been many times that I didn't know if I was taking the right path. I prayed for wisdom and asked God to show me which way to go, and He always came through. This even occurred while writing this book; God has given me clarity on the title and even what I was to write about.

God's guidance comes in different forms, such as intuition, Bible verses, signs, and even people. The Holy Spirit inside of us will often speak to us and let us know whether what we're doing or thinking of doing is good or bad. God has even spoken to me through His word and other people. In the past, people have spoken to me as I've been praying about something, and I knew it was God speaking through them, even though they had no idea.

One thing to always remember is that you're not ever alone; God is always there ready to guide us along our path of righteousness and fulfillment. God will always give you peace and point you in what direction to take. If you have unrest instead of peace, that's a good sign that you are not moving in the right direction. As I've mentioned before, God has specific plans for each of us, and the direction you want to go might not be in God's will for you. So, listen to God and wait for Him to give you peace before moving forward. Believe me, I've gone in my own direction before, even though God didn't give me peace. Each time, I realized I should have listened to God. "If any of you lack wisdom, let him ask of God, that giveth to all men liberally, and upbraideth not, and it shall be given him" (James 1:5). This verse shows us that God is willing to give wisdom and guidance to anyone that asks with a sincere heart. You must always have a sincere heart when asking anything of God because He already knows your true feelings.

This promise of guidance in our lives provides us with much-needed support and direction in our lives. God will give you divine guidance, inspiration, and a sense of purpose in every decision or situation that you face. We should always seek God in prayer and ask Him to lead and guide us and to open doors that only He can open.

There is always something in our lives that requires us to ask important questions or find answers. We constantly need guidance, especially when we're facing important decisions or challenges or seeking a deeper understanding of something. God possesses infinite wisdom and understanding that is far above human comprehension. Trusting God to guide us on our journey of life simply means that we trust God's knowledge more than our own and that we will rely on His wisdom to help us make any decisions that may arise. Through prayer, we talk to God, telling Him our fears, hopes, and dreams, and seek clarity and discernment from Him. We need to have faith that God will guide us to the correct decisions. God's promise of guidance shows us that we need to trust that God has plans for each of our lives and that He will provide the necessary guidance and support to bring His plans into action.

There have been many times when I was at a crossroads and needed to seek God's will for my life. God never fails to come through. When God spoke to me through His Holy Spirit and told me I needed to start writing, I admit I had my doubts. I told God I know nothing about writing, and no one will read what I write. I struggled for almost a year, and then I finally agreed. I told God I needed His help because I know nothing about writing a book. God didn't fail to provide me with all the answers I needed, and He also put people in my life that I needed. God is the one that told me that He would provide the funds for me to fly to California to learn about how to properly write a book. I did hesitate for a minute on that, too, even though I knew God was right. God even had people tell me I needed to go to California, and I'm so glad I listened and went because I came back a different person, ready to become an author. God will give you guidance on any aspect of your life if you simply pray and ask Him for guidance and then listen and obey what He tells you to do. My life is amazing, and I feel so blessed by God as He guides my every step of writing.

This promise of guidance can ultimately result in personal growth, as it did for me, as well as spiritual transformation and character development. God's guidance can lead to inner peace, spiritual enlightenment, and the development of the virtues of compassion, forgiveness, and humility. When I finally submitted to God's will and started writing, my whole life changed for the better, and I believe my outlook on life also changed. I didn't have a bad outlook before, but now I'm more caring and understanding of others. I have more inner peace now than I could have ever imagined. God's guidance may not always align with our desires or expectations, but God's timing is always perfect. He is all-knowing and knows what's best for us in our lives.

We can ask God for guidance through our prayers and seek His answers through our Bible reading and from the prompting of the Holy Spirit. I've had God show me things while I've been reading His word, and other times, the Holy Spirit has spoken to me in dreams. God will speak to you in different ways to give you answers and guidance. My first book was an eBook, and God gave me the title for the book in a dream and then kept speaking the title to me for days. I wanted to make sure it was God telling me the title and not my own thoughts. God can also put people in your pathway and have them say certain words that you know are from God. Sometimes you need to be quiet and listen for that small still voice of the Lord, and He will guide you toward the direction you need to go.

God's promise of guidance is a comforting assurance that goes beyond our human limitations. God's guidance is way deeper than anything we can offer because God's ways are wiser than ours. God can show us guidance through our prayers, meditation, the Bible, and our church. We receive His guidance from the wisdom of our pastor and even through other people that cross our paths. By seeking God, we open ourselves to receiving guidance that will illuminate our path as a shining light, providing clarity in difficult times and even offering peace in moments of uncertainty.

There have been moments in my life when I had no idea what to do, and God gave me peace in my decision. As we talked about before, when you get that peace from God that passes all understanding, you know you're going the right path. There isn't anyone else that can give you so much peace in the face of doubt. It's a great feeling, knowing that God is leading you and you're doing what you need to be doing.

God's promise of guidance lets us know that our path of life may not always be smooth or clear, and there may be challenges, roadblocks, detours, and unexpected turns along the way. However, by trusting God and having faith, we can find strength and direction, knowing that He is with us every step of the way.

The beginning of this year started out for me with an unexpected turn in the form of my precious Aunt leaving this world. We had gotten closer than ever the few months before because she had been sick, and I was trying to take care of her. It felt like I wasn't in my right mind for a few months after she passed, and I was stuck on a dead-end road. Yet God was still there helping me get back on the highway to where I needed to be. So, no matter what detours you face, remember God is always there ready to help. Just reach out for His hand to help you.

God's promise of guidance doesn't guarantee us a problem-free life, but His presence and support. He will guide us through difficult decisions, offer comfort in times of sorrow, and inspire us to make choices that are in alignment with His will. By seeking God's guidance and surrendering ourselves to His infinite wisdom, we will be able to navigate life's path with a sense of purpose and deepened faith in His plan for us.

Earlier we talked about the importance of having a purpose in life. With God by your side, you will always have a life that is filled with purpose. We must remember that God's promise of guidance shows us that we are cherished and loved and that we can always turn to Him for help and direction if we lose sight of that purpose.

We need to have an intimate relationship with Jesus and not just seek Him when we're having problems. God is not our spare tire to use in emergencies; He's our friend that sticks closer than a brother, who will always be by our side during good times and bad. He has promised to never leave you or forsake you. The best friend you will ever find is the Lord Jesus Christ. "A man that hath friends must shew himself friendly: And there is a friend that sticketh closer than a brother" (Proverbs 18:24).

We need to trust in God's guidance as we navigate all the complexities of life, and there will be plenty of them. God's promise of guidance shows us that God is not only the creator of the universe but also a compassionate and loving guide for His creation. "Even every one that is called by my name: for I have created him for my glory, I have formed him; yea, I have made him" (Isaiah 43:7).

In times of confusion or decision-making, God's promise of guidance provides us with a sense of direction and clarity. God's guidance also extends to moral and ethical choices we may be faced with, helping us navigate the complexities of right and wrong. God's promise of guidance is an invitation to fully trust in Him and His plans for our lives, to seek His infinite wisdom, and to rely on His love and support. By having an intimate relationship with the Lord Jesus Christ, we are able to find purpose, peace, and fulfillment along the way.

CHAPTER 6

PROMISE OF STRENGTH:

Overcoming Challenges

But those who hope in the Lord will renew their strength.
They will soar on wings like eagles; they will run and not grow
weary; they will walk and not faint. Isaiah 40:31

We've already talked about a lot of God's promises, and in this chapter, we will be talking about the promise of strength. This is another promise I love because nobody wants to feel weak or unable to get through something. We can be assured that God will always be there to help us and give us strength. We will always be going through some trial or situation in our lives, so it's reassuring to know that we have our Lord Jesus Christ to give us strength in whatever we might be dealing with.

God might not always remove your problems; however, He will show you a way to get through them. I was talking to a friend the other day who was going through some trials, and she told me she just wants God to tell her what to do. My response to her was to keep praying for God to give her wisdom. You might be in a situation like my friend and not know which direction to go. God has your trial or situation already taken care of, but He wants you to pray and talk to Him about it. He will give you the strength to get through anything, and He will give you the wisdom to know what to do.

You might be thinking that you have already prayed and are still praying, but you're not getting any answers. My friend told me this too, and I told her that maybe God wants her to be still and wait or maybe listen for His small still voice to tell her something. God is working in the background a lot of times when we think He's not speaking to us or answering our prayers. It's hard to wait, but sometimes God just wants us to wait.

Believe me, I know all about waiting on God. There have been numerous times that I have prayed, and God has told me to wait. God wasn't saying no, yes, or even maybe. There's never a maybe with God because He knows exactly what He is going to do. "Wait on the Lord: be of good courage, and He shall strengthen thine heart: wait, I say, on the Lord" (Psalms 27:14). When you're waiting on the Lord, just know He's working for your benefit to prepare everything for you. If you think God is silent, just remember that even a teacher is silent during a test. God sees over the rainbow, so keep looking up and waiting on God to show up at just the right time.

As I mentioned before, I was once about to run out of unemployment but still hadn't gotten a job offer from the many interviews I had gone on. Then God showed up, and I started a new job as my unemployment was ending. God never fails and will always be there to help hold you up and give you strength in any situation. "Be still and know that I am God: I will be exalted among the heathen, I will be exalted in the earth" (Psalms 46:10).

Sometimes when we're waiting on God, we need to be still and hear Him speaking to us through the Holy Spirit. If you are anything like me, you are not a patient person, and waiting and being still requires being patient. However, the results are amazing when you are still and listen to God. God's promise of strength gives us encouragement and comfort in navigating life's difficulties as He helps us rise above any situation.

Our lives are so busy and full of distractions that I think sometimes God requires us to get away from all the noise to concentrate on Him and hear what He's telling us. He will speak to our hearts through His Holy Spirit, but we must be willing to listen. There are days when my husband has the TV on and my phone is going off with texts and social media notifications, so I just go outside and sit underneath our Bradford pear tree in the backyard or take a walk down the street to get some peace and quiet, leaving my phone inside the house. Sometimes it seems that God is closer to me when I'm outside with nature, whether I'm planting flowers, sitting underneath our tree, or walking around the neighborhood. I go outside and talk to the flowers or the birds flying around the bird bath, and I can hear God more clearly because it's quiet and there are no distractions. If I have something on my mind, you will usually find me outside looking up to the Heavens and talking to God. It's good to be able to talk to the Great Creator, who will help me with any problems or questions I may have. There isn't a life challenge that is too big or too hard for our God. Always remember that God is bigger than whatever problem you may be facing.

God's promise of strength gives us hope and encouragement. God assures us that He will give us the necessary strength to overcome whatever life throws at us. "I can do all things through Christ who strengthens me" (Philippians 4:13).

I mentioned my aunt passing before, which was a very hard time for me. It was a time that I needed to rely on God's strength like never before, and He never failed. I knew she had gone from this life to a better life, but it happened so suddenly that I was still lost and needed strength to go on with my own life. I called out to my Lord Jesus Christ, and He gave me incredible strength every day. Like the song says, "I need you every hour." That song became so true in my life at the beginning of this year. Trust God, and He will give you the strength to get through anything, even death. To say it's easy now isn't true; however, God makes it easier because when I feel weak, He makes me strong. I'm at my strongest when I'm leaning on Jesus and when He is holding my hand helping me, and He does every day.

There are numerous stories in the Bible that talk about people who faced insurmountable challenges but found strength in God to overcome them. Think about Moses and the Israelites in the Old Testament in Exodus. This is a good example of how God gave strength to overcome what seemed to be impossible odds. Despite the numerous obstacles they faced, such as crossing the Red Sea, God gave them strength and guidance and led them to the Promised Land. "And the children of the Israel went into the midst of the sea upon the dry ground: and the waters were a wall upon them on their right hand, and on their left" (Exodus 14:22). If God can turn the Red Sea into dry ground for the Israelites, imagine what He can do for you and me. God didn't remove the Red Sea. He parted it. God doesn't always remove your problems, but He will forge a way through them.

The life of Jesus Christ serves as a powerful example for us of strength in the face of adversity. Through His teachings, miracles, and ultimate sacrifice on the cross, Jesus displayed unwavering strength and triumphed over sin and death. His resurrection shows us the promise of victory over challenges and serves as a source of hope for us. It shows us that no matter what we face on this earth, there isn't anything that our Lord God hasn't already faced, and He is able and willing to give us the strength we need to conquer anything.

While we are on this earth, we will face trials and even tribulations, and we will need strength from God. There will be people who let you down and break your heart. In times like that, remember that God is always there for you to help you get through anything. Most of us have heard the saying that God will not give us more than we can handle; however, when we're going through a lot, we don't see our strength as God sees it. God sees us as stronger than we really think we are.

I've been through a lot in the past few years, as I have had a lot of friends and family leave this earth to a better place in Heaven.

My strength didn't feel that strong, but now I see how strong of a person God has helped me become. It may take time – it has been a process for me – but God will help you get where you need to be. "Thy shoes shall be iron and brass; and as thy days, so shall thy strength be" (Deuteronomy 33:25). This verse explains that your strength will equal your days, so always remember your strength will increase every time God helps you face a bump in the road.

There was a span of two years where there was always something plaguing our family, whether sickness, death, or something else terrible. My family and every one of my dad's siblings' families had something going on, so we were all wondering why this was happening to us and what was going to happen next. Other people even noticed and began to comment on how much we were dealing with, and one of my aunts even said that our family has a black cloud over it.

Eventually I realized that God was taking care of us through it all. Thinking back on that time, God might have been strengthening our family. Maybe God was using us to show others how much strength we had and how we were getting through it with our faith.

God wants us to be dependent on Him and to rely on His strength rather than our own. We might think that we have enough strength on our own, but we don't. If you have strength as you're going through something, it's because God is giving it to you. God has enough strength for every storm that we may face in our life. It's God's grace that provides us enough strength to get through every day. "And He said unto me, My grace is sufficient for thee: for my strength is made perfect in weakness. Most gladly therefore will I rather glory in my infirmities, that the power of Christ may rest upon me" (2 Corinthians 12:9). God's power being made perfect is what sustains us and gets us through every weakness that we encounter. Our human strength will fail us every day, but God's strength will never fail and is renewed every morning. You can't count on anything in this world, but you can count on God's strength to be there when you need it.

When you face challenges and don't know what to do, turn to God and ask Him to give you the strength you need, and He will. "These things I have spoken unto you, that in me ye might have peace. In the world, ye shall have tribulation: but be of good cheer; I have overcome the world" (John 16:33). God is a source of refuge and strength; He is always ready to assist and empower you with His strength. By trusting God, seeking His help, and relying on Him, you can obtain a wellspring of inner strength to be able to face life challenges, overcome obstacles, and persevere through difficult circumstances.

God is omnipotent, meaning He possesses unlimited power. This power extends not only to the creation of the universe but also to upholding and sustaining it. You can rest on the fact that the same God that created Heaven and Earth is also your source of strength.

God's promise of strength comes from God's nature as a loving and all-powerful God. You can find assurance in knowing that God is not only aware of your challenges but also working on your behalf. The Holy Spirit is also a source of strength that enables you to live out your faith and overcome obstacles in fulfilling God's purpose.

God's promise of strength is a source of comfort, encouragement, and guidance, and it assures us that we are never alone in this life.

CHAPTER 7

PROMISE OF PEACE:

Tranquility Amidst Chaos

Peace I leave with you, my peace I give unto you: not as the world giveth, give I unto you. Let not your heart be troubled, neither let it be afraid. John 14:27

Now we are going to talk about God's promise of peace. What does peace mean to you? Is it peace and quiet from a noisy place, or is it much deeper? Webster defines peace as "a state of tranquility or quiet; harmony in personal relations; freedom from disquieting or oppressive thoughts or emotions; a state or period of mutual concord between governments."

There are many ways to describe peace in our world and in our personal lives, but how does God describe peace? After all, He is the One that gives it to us. The Biblical meaning of peace is knowing that the Lord of our universe is by your side. Peace is sitting in comfort and knowing that God is by your side no matter what. Perfect peace is when we are whole and complete, and you can achieve perfect peace by focusing on Jesus.

God's promise of peace is a source of comfort and hope that offers reassurance in times of turmoil in our lives. You can receive inner peace through faith, compassion, forgiveness, and understanding. Jesus is the Prince of Peace, and through faith in Jesus, you can experience peace with God and have a new or restored relationship with Him. Inner peace will give you a sense of tranquility that extends to all your relationships.

God's promise of peace is comprehensive in that it encompasses personal peace through reconciliation with God, inner tranquility, harmonious relationships, comfort in times of trouble, and the hope of a future world without strife. It is a promise that offers us guidance, strength, and the assurance of God's loving presence in our lives. The Holy Spirit will help you experience peace in your heart and live a peaceful life full of love, joy, patience, kindness, and goodness. The peace of God is like no other peace; there aren't even words to describe it.

God is all-powerful and omnipresent, omnipotent, and miraculous. He has given us all these promises in His Word and He loves us so much that He will fulfil all these promises in our lives. God is our refuge and strength and a present help in times of trouble. It's so much better to go through this life with God on your side.

There have been times I had been going through a crisis, and I felt God's presence right by my side. He's always with me and gives me the peace of knowing that I'm doing the right thing. If you don't feel peace, God is telling you to go in a different direction. Listen to

God speak to your heart, and He will always give you peace about all the decisions in your life. If Daniel can trust God in the lion's den, then you should trust God in your life's journey. God always sees what we can't see. He is always working behind the scenes to transform, redeem, and resurrect lives. He has the power to change your life and destiny. Trust Him with your life and see how much peace He will give you.

God's promise of peace is a significant aspect of faith. Throughout the Bible, God assures you of His desire for peace both in your relationship with Him and in the world. "Thou will keep Him in perfect peace, whose mind is stayed on thee: because He trusteth in thee" (Isaiah 26:3). Through faith in Jesus and following His teachings in the Bible, you can experience the peace of God, even with life's challenges and uncertainties. We can trust in God's faithfulness and love and be assured that He will fulfill His promise of peace to you.

Through faith in Jesus Christ, you can be reconciled with God and have peace in your relationship with Him. This peace comes from the forgiveness of sins and the assurance of eternal life in God's presence. By accepting Jesus as your Savior, you will receive salvation and the gift of peace with God.

We all know that our lives can be filled with challenges, trials, and tribulations at times. Be assured that God is with you in all your struggles. "These things I have spoken unto you, that in Me ye might have peace. In the world ye shall have tribulation: but be of good cheer; I have overcome the world" (John 16:33). You can find peace in knowing that God's peace and strength is available to you whenever you need it. He's waiting on you to call on Him and ask for His help. The Holy Spirit that indwells in you will also provide guidance, comfort, and peace. Through the Holy Spirit working in your heart, you can experience a transformative peace in your thoughts, actions, and emotions. When we put our problems in God's hands, He puts peace in our hearts.

We all want to live in harmony and unity with everyone. To live in peace with others, you will need to love your neighbors, seek reconciliation, and promote peace in your relations with others. We are all born with a sinful nature and separated from God. God's promise of peace is realized through Jesus Christ, who reconciles humanity to God. With the Holy Spirit, you can experience a deep sense of tranquility, contentment, and harmony. This inner peace is beyond human understanding and guards your heart and mind. This peace is the only way that we can live harmoniously with others while we're living on this earth. "And the peace of God, which passeth all understanding, shall keep your hearts and minds through Christ Jesus" (Philippians 4:7). By relying on God's promises and trusting His faithfulness, you can find peace amid adversity.

The Holy Spirit, who is the presence of God within you, will empower and guide you on your journey of faith. The Holy Spirit will produce the fruit of peace in your life, allowing you to exhibit peace in your relationships, decisions, and attitudes. You can experience a deep sense of serenity and calmness. Jesus is called the Prince of Peace because He will give you such a deep feeling of peace within yourself in times of despair and trouble that it's indescribable. Are you fretting over something in your life? Let Jesus take care of it and let Him give you that calming peace.

God's promise of peace includes peace with God, inner peace, peace through salvation, peace in difficult situations, peace through the Holy Spirit, peace in your community, and the ultimate peace in God's Kingdom. This promise of peace provides comfort, assurance, and being able to live as God's children in this world as we pass through to our Heavenly home. God promises perfect peace to those who put their trust in Him. This world will not and cannot give you the peace that God will give you because it is too fragile and too unstable. The peace that comes from God is a personal peace that affects your heart and soul regardless of your circumstances or what you may be going through. When you feel like your world is crumbling around you, God is there to offer you His peace.

Peace is something that everyone wants but few will get because they don't have faith and trust in God. Peace is directly related to the actions and attitudes of people, and it ultimately is a gift from God. The presence of peace is truly a blessing from God for our obedience to Him. We all have a choice to either trust God's promises and let His peace rule our lives or rely on ourselves and reject the peace God offers. Peace is a fruit of the Spirit, so if we allow the Spirit of God to rule our lives, then we will experience God's peace. God will give His peace to those who trust Him, and once His peace rules in our hearts, we will be able to share it with others.

God promised to bless the Israelites before they entered the Promised Land if they obeyed and served Him. He promised to protect them and to give them peace, and He promises the same thing for us today. In every situation that we face, God has promised to free us from anxiety, worry, doubt, and fear. God wants to see you prosper, and He wants to bless you abundantly.

How many times do we let things in our lives dominate our mind and thoughts? Situations have entirely consumed me before, causing me to fret and worry until I realized it was Satan in my head. Then I prayed for God to help me, and He gave me peace. Satan wants to keep us worrying about things. He wants us to forget that God can and will take care of our problems and give us peace about them. Our lives shouldn't be dominated by circumstances outside our control, so turn them over to God and let Him give you peace.

We need to start by focusing on God and reading and studying His Word. We must realize that God wants us to be healthy, happy, and free from worry. "Now the Lord of peace Himself give you peace always by all means. The Lord be with you all" (2 Thessalonians 3:16). Declare to yourself and believe that God's promises are true, and they are for you. Don't allow yourself to be dominated by worries, problems, or fears, and don't give in to distractions. Seek to be faithful to God and spend time with Him by reading His Word, praying, and seeking Him until He gives you peace. God is our Lord of peace.

The peace offered by the world is an empty promise; it will only bring temporary peace. However, God's peace is permanent and is offered by the only One that can be trusted to keep His promises. The world's peace is fleeting and changes with every circumstance. We all know that to solve a problem, we must get to the root of it instead of just putting a band-aid over it. The world's peace also ignores the root of the problem. But God's peace is permanent and grounded in His Word. His peace doesn't change with the circumstances; it is secure no matter what.

The world's peace is described as life without conflict; however, God's peace is something different. God's peace is tranquility in any and every circumstance. Jesus will offer you His peace, but it's an offer, and you must accept it to receive it. You must have faith and believe and trust that God will give you peace in your life no matter what you're going through. Trust God and call out to Him to help you, and He will give you peace that is beyond human understanding.

Biblical peace is a state of calm; it is freedom from strife or discord and creates harmony in personal relationships. God's peace and the world's peace are completely different. Jesus is our answer to the soul-wrenching peace we all desire to have. When we make peace with God and have faith in Him, we will experience the peace that only comes from belief in Jesus.

You can only experience that peace if you have an intimate relationship with Jesus. We have best friends on this earth, but we all need to make Jesus our best friend. He should be the One we call out to when we have a need. He shouldn't be second fiddle to our friends or family. I make this mistake, too; many times I have talked to my friends and family about a situation before I talked to God, despite knowing that He is the only one that can truly intervene and take care of it. God wants us to call out to Him about our problems even though He already knows all about them. He wants to hear from us. Remember, don't wait until you're falling apart to call out to God. Reach out Him before you reach your breaking point. Freedom comes when you release your problems and worries, and with freedom comes peace, so turn those problems into prayers. Peace is a gift and a fruit we bear. Finding the peace that Jesus offers may not be easy, but it's always accessible to us. No matter your circumstance or what you may be going through, it is possible to find the undeniable peace of God that we all crave.

CHAPTER 8

PROMISE OF HEALING:

Restoring Of Wholeness

Heal me, O Lord, and I shall be healed; save me, and I shall be
saved; for thou art my praise. Jeremiah 17:14

There are still a lot more of God's promises that we haven't talked about, so I hope you will study God's Word and find the rest. I hope by now you can see how faithful God is to us with not only His promises to us daily but in every aspect of our lives. We need to have faith and trust in God and have a relationship with Him to get the full potential of all His promises. We all need to try and be more faithful to God since He's so faithful to us and takes care of us and all our needs and wants.

Now let's talk about His healing promise. This is a big promise because so many people are sick or suffer from disease. When I was growing up, I don't think I remember people being as sick as I see them now. Maybe it's the food we eat. Growing up we had a garden, where much of our food came from. Who ever heard of opening a can of food or microwaving a meal? I can only imagine what they are putting in our food nowadays, and most of us use a microwave, potentially exposing us to radiation. We sure didn't go out to a restaurant to eat except for special occasions, and even then, we mostly got together with the family over a big meal at the grandparents' house.

No matter how much sickness is in the world, God is the Great Healer and the Great Physician. God's promise of healing doesn't only apply to sickness; it can also apply to healing a broken heart or spiritual wounds. Wherever you need healing, God will fulfill His promise of healing and fulfil your needs. Webster's definition of healing is "to make free from injury or disease; to make sound or whole; to make well again." The Biblical definition of healing is to make solid or whole; the restoration of health in making whole or well physically, mentally, or spiritually.

We have talked before about how God cares about the whole person, and His healing promise isn't just to heal you physically; it's to heal you in all aspects of your life. "And the prayer of faith shall save the sick, and the Lord shall raise him up; and if he have committed sins, they shall be forgiven him" (James 5:15). "For I will restore health unto thee, and I will heal thee of thy wounds, saith the Lord...." (Jeremiah 30:17).

Faith, prayer, and trust in God's plan are essential in understanding His Will when it comes to His promise of healing physically. "Therefore, I say unto you, what things soever ye desire, when ye pray, believe that ye receive them, and ye shall have them" (Mark 11:24). We need unwavering faith when seeking healing through prayer. However, many times, we pray for someone to be healed of their sickness, but it isn't God's plan to heal them on Earth. Instead, he heals them by taking them to Heaven. We must rest in God's promise and know that they were healed in God's way and not our way. God's way is always much better than ours in everything.

I had a friend years ago that had cancer for nearly five years, if not more. She went through chemo, numerous tests, and other treatments. She was indeed a fighter and a strong person, and her faith was always in God. The day came that God took her home to be with Him in Heaven, and my heart was crushed. It took me a little while to realize that we were being selfish wanting her to stay here dealing with cancer. God healed her when He took her to Heaven, and she no longer had any cancer or any pain at all.

Then, the first of this year, God took my aunt to Heaven after she was diagnosed with cancer. God really had to heal my heart after she left this earth, and He did. My Aunt found out about two weeks before she passed that she had a cancer that had spread throughout her body. The doctors gave her several months, but they didn't know God's plan.

My aunt had always had some kind of sickness that started in her childhood. No matter how sick she was, she always talked about Jesus and always went to church. Her trust was in God, and she knew she would go to Heaven when she left this earth. On her last few days, I told her that God could still heal her body and she told me that He wasn't going to do that. It was like she knew He would heal her by taking her to Heaven. My heart was totally crushed when she left because we were close. I didn't know what to do without her, so I put my loss in God's hands, and over time, He healed my heart. In the process, I could feel God with me every day. God will be with you always while you heal. Trust God and lean on Him to take care of you, give you wisdom, and direct your path.

God's promise of healing shows us that God is a loving and compassionate Heavenly Father who cares for His Children's well-being. God is willing and able to heal and restore those who are suffering physically, emotionally, and spiritually. God has been with me and helped me in all those areas of my life at one time or another.

In Exodus 15:26, God tells the Israelites, "...I am the Lord that healeth thee." After the Israelites left Egypt, God revealed himself as their healer and protector. God is also our healer and protector, and He wants you to trust Him and believe that He will heal and protect you in good times and bad.

There are numerous times in the Bible where Jesus performed acts of healing. He accomplished several miracles, such as restoring sight to the blind, making the lame walk, and curing those with various diseases. Don't tell me that God can't heal you, because He can and will if that's His Will for your life.

God is the Great Miracle Worker. He healed me of my cancer 14 years ago. So many people had cancer worse than me, yet God let mine be small, and I only had to go through radiation. My mom, on the other hand, and another aunt had it much worse. My mom had it three times and underwent chemo and radiation as well as surgery. The doctors told us she was in stage 3, maybe 4, and it had spread through her lymph nodes. I can say that God is a miracle worker because, after lots of prayer to God, my mom has been cancer-free almost six years now. God is willing and able to perform miracles in your life as well; all you need to do is call out to Him in prayer and faith, believing that He will, and He will supply all your needs. God's divine power and compassion is available to all who seek Him through faith.

God will also heal through the anointing of oil on a sick person. I've been in church and seen the anointing of oil and prayer for healing, and God will always show up and heal if it's His Will. God wants us to believe that healing will happen, whether it happens here on Earth or in heaven, and He wants us to trust Him fully with all our hearts and souls. God promises healing and He will fulfill His promise; however, His Will and timing might not be in line with our immediate desires. Some may receive instant healing, while others may experience healing through a gradual process and may even find peace and strength in their suffering. Even others may not be healed on this earth but will be healed when they go to Heaven. God may even take them home to heaven sooner than we expect to heal them. Trusting in God's plan and purpose is crucial, knowing that He works all things together for the good in our lives. "And we know that all things work together for good to them that love God, to them who are the called according to His purpose" (Romans 8:28).

God's healing also extends beyond physical ailments to the brokenness and pain within a person's mind and heart. Most have us have experienced a tragic event, which can cause our minds to become so wrapped around the circumstances that we almost can't function. You might have also had someone hurt you so badly that your heart felt like it had broken into a billion pieces.

There was a time several years ago when life got so rough that I went into a state of depression. That just wasn't me because I was always laughing and smiling and enjoying life. Through lots of prayers from myself, family members, and friends, God raised me up out of that depression. You can never go so far or so deep into depression that God cannot reach you and restore you. Sometimes people do have a chemical imbalance in their brain that causes depression, but mine wasn't that; it was Satan. Satan is always around trying to cause problems in our lives so we will stop having faith in God. Satan might think he's winning, but it won't be for long.

After God restored me from my depression, I was back being my happy, joyful self, and I've never had a bout of depression since. I hope you can see the process I've been trying to show you. God is always faithful to us, and all He wants from us is our faith and trust in Him. Life will always throw you curveballs but isn't it great knowing that we have a God that is always looking out for us and taking care of us?

God's healing promise is for the person as a whole because of the sin that's in our world. Sin has caused brokenness and suffering, and it affects not only our bodies but also our relationships with others, our emotions, and our spiritual well-being. God's promise of healing is connected to God's compassion and love for those who are suffering. God cares about your pain and is present with you during your struggles. God is always close to the brokenhearted. "God is our refuge and strength, a very present help in trouble" (Psalms 46:1). God's ability to bring comfort and healing offers hope and strength during difficult times.

We should always pray for others – not just ourselves – that need God's healing power in their lives. To be able to pray for others and lift them up to the throne room of God will not only help their healing but will also help encourage you. Your journey of healing may also require patience and trusting God's timing and plan. Lean on God's promises, stay steadfast in your faith, and find hope and encouragement to persevere through any challenges this world throws at you.

God's Will is not always for instant healing like we want, so you must seek God and His infinite wisdom and guidance to understand His purpose and Will in your individual circumstances. God can bring supernatural healing if it's in His plan; however, sometimes, God will use doctors and nurses and medicine to bring healing. God is in control, so even though it was the medicine the doctors gave you that healed you, remember it was God's healing hand that was on you, and it was God that gave the doctors wisdom to help in your healing process. God's promise of healing shows us that God is a compassionate and loving God who desires for the well-being of His people. He wants us to trust Him, seek His presence in times of need, and experience His transformative power in all aspects of our life.

God's healing is on an individual basis and will be different for each person according to his specific plan for them. In the healing process, you will receive the hope of redemption, restoration, and eternal life.

There is also a link between spiritual and physical healing. Forgiveness is important and has an impact on your overall well-being. Healing isn't only due to our own efforts; it is in God's hands. Acknowledging our own limitations and humbly surrendering to God's Will and timing is crucial. God's promise of healing will also heal past wounds and hurts, and you will be able to experience freedom from the burdens of your past. Through prayer and faith, you can find hope, comfort, and strength to face life's challenges, knowing that God's love and grace are ever present and always with you.

CHAPTER 9

PROMISE OF LOVE:

Embracing Unconditional Affection

Beloved, let us love one another: for love is of God; and everyone that loveth is born of God, and knoweth God. He that loveth not knoweth not God; for God is love. I John 4:7-8

People say "I love you" all the time, and sometimes you wonder if they really mean what they say. Do they even know the true meaning of love? Do any of us really know? You've heard the saying that love is in the air. Well, something is in the air, but the question is whether it's true love.

We love with all our hearts, but we can't love unconditionally because we hold people responsible for things. You might tell your husband you love him and really mean it, but then he does something you don't like, and you yell at him. Do you still love him, or is your love based on how he acts? As I mentioned before, I'm a people person. I like watching people and how they act and interact with others. If only we could have unconditional love toward others like Jesus; oh, what a different world we could live in. We're not able to do that, though, and only God is able to show unconditional love.

The definition of love according to Webster is "strong affection for another arising out of kinship or personal ties; affection based on admiration, or common interest." Love according to the Bible is God because God is love. He isn't just loving; He is the very definition of love, and that's why there is no easy way to describe God's love. He both generates and demonstrates love to us, and His love is unconditional and endures forever. "For God so loved the world that He gave his only begotten Son, that whosoever believes in Him should not perish but have eternal life" (John 3:16).

God's love is seen as a powerful force that offers forgiveness, redemption, and salvation to believers. It is not based on anything but is freely given to all who have faith and believe in God. The Bible shows us that God's love is evident in Him creating the world and everything in it. The beauty and complexities of nature can be seen as God illustrating His love for His creations.

God's love is compassionate and merciful, and He shows patience and understanding toward our weaknesses, offering forgiveness and giving second chances to those that repent. God desires a personal relationship with each of us. Through prayer, worship, and studying His Word, you can experience God's love and guidance. God's ultimate expression of love for all humanity was seen in the sacrificial love of Jesus, who willingly gave up His life for the salvation of humanity. Really think about this for a moment. God loves you unconditionally.

He loves you so much that His Son Jesus Christ died on the cruel cross of Calvary and rose again on the third day so you could have an eternal home in Heaven one day. Now that's love. Have you thanked Him for loving us unconditionally and so much more than we deserve? We're not able to love unconditionally, so it's hard for us to understand.

God even loves those that oppose Him and don't want anything to do with Him. I'm sure we were all taught as children to love our enemies and pray for them. When you do this, you are showing God's boundless love for all humanity. God's love never changes and remains the same. No matter what circumstances arise or what mistakes we make, God's love is steadfast. Knowing this will give you a sense of security and comfort. When you're going through issues in life and think no one loves you, remember God loves you and always will. He's the same yesterday, today, and tomorrow. God's promise of love serves as a foundation for faith, hope, and purpose and will give you encouragement for your day so that you may share God's love with others. "But God commended His love toward us, in that, while we were still sinners, Christ died for us" (Romans 5:8).

God's promise of love also includes the offer of redemption and forgiveness to all who will seek it sincerely. God's love is patient and long-suffering, enduring through the ages despite our shortcomings. God is patient, but we are not, so God must teach it to us. God's desire is for all people to come to repentance; he shows His loving patience in giving people time to turn toward Him. "The Lord is not slack concerning His promise, as some men count slackness; but is longsuffering to us-ward, not willing that any should perish, but that all should come to repentance" (2 Peter 3:9).

God's love extends to all people regardless of their race, nationality, or background. At the foot of the cross we are all counted equal in the sight of God. In the world today, if you are of a different color or religion, you might be treated differently – but not with God. After all, God created us all, so He should view us all as equal. Why can't we do that? This world would be a much better place. Black Lives Matter, White Lives Matter – All Lives Matter to Jesus.

We must show the love of Jesus to everyone if we're going to make any kind of change in this world we live in. God's promise of love brings about unconditional love, sacrificial redemption, loving relationships, forgiveness, and a willingness to love others. It serves as a beacon of hope and guidance, inspiring you to live in harmony with God's Will and to share His love with the world. We must constantly share God's love with others so that other people can experience it and the peace and joy that comes with it.

God's love is eternal and unchanging. It transcends time and remains constant throughout all generations. So, the love of God that our great-grandparents had is the same love that God shows us today. "O give thanks unto the God of heaven: for His mercy endureth forever" (Psalms 136:26). We should all be thankful that God loves us so much that He promises to always be there for us. As humans, we can't always promise to help and be faithful to our family and friends, but God can and does. God's love can shape us from the inside and out because if our spiritual needs are met, then our bodies, souls, and spirits will be in line with God.

The word Christian simply means Christ-like. So many people don't strive to be Christ-like and want to live their lives their way without even talking to their Heavenly Father. We have an earthly father, and a lot of times we emulate that figure in our lives. So why can't we follow the ways of the Heavenly Father? Let's appreciate the love of our Heavenly Father and not take it for granted.

Why does God love us? Have you ever thought about that? I'm sure you heard growing up that God loves you and have probably even heard the song "Jesus Loves You." So, let's explore why. First, God loves us because God is Holy, and He is filled with an infinite measure of Holy, pure, and indescribable love. Secondly, God loves us because He created us in His image. We are God's children, and we are important to Him. Those of you that have children know what it is to love them. God loves us as His children; however, His love toward us is much more perfect. "For God so loved the world that He gave His only begotten Son that whosoever believes in Him might not perish but have everlasting life" (John 3:16). Who do you know that would give up their life and die for someone? Would you die for your family? God is the only one who would send their Son to die for you.

God's love gives meaning and purpose to our lives and helps us see that our lives have value and significance. God loves all people no matter their background or social status, so we need to love like God and treat all people with respect and compassion no matter what. "He that loveth not knoweth not God; for God is love" (I John 4:8). Let us all love others like God loves others. Don't look on the outside; see what is on the inside.

We don't earn God's love by doing any certain action, and we're not good enough to even earn His love. God loves us not because of who we are but because of who He is. God is love, and because it is His very nature, He must demonstrate it. God's love is different than our love. God's love is agape love, the love of self-sacrifice. He sacrificed by sending his love to the cross to pay the penalty for our sins, even though we didn't deserve it.

God's love is also personal. He knows every one of us individually; He knows our name, and He loves us personally. God's love is powerful and has no beginning and no end. There are some days we might love someone and other days we might not love them at all, depending on their actions or how we are feeling; however, God will love you every day until the end of time.

God loves you so much because of who He is: He is love. His laws and actions flow out of who He is, and we associate good with God because of who He is and bad with Satan because of who he is. God's love for us will never change because God never changes, and even at our worst, God will still love us. God will let us reap what we sow and demands that we repent of our sins, but God also shows us mercy and grace with His love.

God also loves you because it brings Him glory. God is most glorified in us when we are most satisfied in Him. Because God is committed to His own glory, God is just as committed to loving us. God created us for His glory, so when He shows us His love, forgives us of our sins, and blesses us when we don't deserve it, a light shines onto His greatness. The phrase "give God praise and glory" is about glorifying God for all that He has done for us, from creating us to blessing us daily.

God also wants us to love others like He loves us. He commands us to love Him, love ourselves, and love others. "And we have known and believed the love that God had to us. God is love; and he that dwelleth in love dwelleth in God, and God in him. We love Him because He first loved us" (I John 4:16,19). God told us to love everyone like he loved us; however, sometimes that is hard, especially if it's someone that has hurt you or someone that is just a mean person. It might be that these people need Jesus, so you can show them love by showing them Jesus.

God loves you more than you can imagine. He created you to love Him and to share His love with people around you. But God will not force His love on you, even though he loves the entire world. He will only save those that believe in Him. So, wherever you go on your journey of life, remember to always show God's love to others and tell them about the love of Jesus. You will be amazed how blessed you will feel by spreading love around.

CHAPTER 10

PROMISE OF ETERNAL LIFE:

Hope Beyond The Present

But whosever drinketh of the water that I shall give him shall never thirst; but the water that I shall give him shall be in him a well of water springing up into everlasting life. John 4:14

It is not time to talk about the most important promise of all: the promise of eternal life. I consider this the most important because one day we will leave this earth and where you go for eternity depends on you and the choices you make while on earth. It's not whether you make good or bad choices; it's whether you accept God's love. Like we talked about in the previous chapter, God loves us all, but he won't force you to love Him. If you want to spend eternity with God, who created, loved, and took care of you on this earth, then you will have to accept Him as your Lord and Savior before you leave it.

What does eternal mean to you? Webster's definition of eternal is "having infinite duration; continued without intermission; seemingly endless; existing at all times; and characterized by abiding fellowship with God." Even Webster associates the word eternal with being in fellowship with God. The biblical definition of eternal is "without beginning or end of existence; everlasting, endless, immortal." It may be hard to think about being somewhere for eternity, but it will happen to us someday. You never know when your last day on Earth will be because we are not promised tomorrow. I'm thankful every morning when I awake to see that God has given me yet another day because I know my purpose on Earth isn't finished. God has a purpose for all of us, and until that purpose is complete, you will be on this earth – unless God decides it's time to take you home to be with Him.

Eternal life isn't just living forever; it is living forever in the presence of God Almighty. God created you and wanted you to live with Him forever. That's why He sent Jesus to die on the cruel cross to pay the ransom for your sins. God promises eternal life, and just like you can't do anything to earn God's love, you can't do anything to earn eternal life. The promise of eternal life is a gift from God that He graciously gives us. You can receive this gift of eternal life by trusting not in your own righteousness but in the one person that never sinned, Jesus Christ, God's only Son, who was the perfect substitute for our sin. "For the wages of sin is death; but the gift of God is eternal life through Jesus Christ our Lord" (Romans 6:23).

You might not think you sin because you haven't killed anyone, but we sin every day because we're not perfect. God is the only one that is perfect and cannot sin.

God's promise of eternal life is for those that believe in Jesus and believe that He rose again the third day. We cannot fix ourselves; that's the purpose of Jesus suffering as payment for our sins. All you need to do to accept this promise of eternal life is to admit that you're a sinner and acknowledge that you need a Savior.

God's Word is life-changing in His many promises. God has promises of real love, forgiveness, salvation, peace, hope, and joy for everyone who puts their trust in Jesus Christ. "Surely goodness and mercy shall follow me all the days of my life: And I will dwell in the house of the Lord forever" (Psalms 23:6). Eternal life is a source of hope, comfort, and assurance, encouraging us to live our lives guided by faith and a relationship with God.

The only way to receive eternal life is through faith in Jesus Christ as God's Son and Savior of the world. Jesus sacrificing Himself on the cross reconciled humanity with God and offered forgiveness of sins. By accepting salvation through faith in Jesus, we're promised eternal life. Don't think that eternal life will be just an extension of our earthly life. On earth there is sin, but in Heaven, there will be no sin and you will be in a state of spiritual perfection. You will be free from sin, suffering, and death. You will have an intimate relationship with God and will experience His love, joy, and peace forever.

One day when God says it's time, Jesus will return to this earth, and we will return with Him to Heaven. That's when those that have already died will be raised from the dead and transformed into spiritual bodies. The resurrection of the saints is when the soul and body are reunited in a glorified form. The promise of eternal life assures us that death is not the end of the road but a transition to a new and everlasting life with God. This hope is an encouragement to persevere in our faith and live according to God's Word. There is a final judgement where we all will be held accountable for our actions and choices. Those who have accepted God's gift of salvation will inherit eternal life, while those who have rejected it will face eternal separation from God with torments in Hell. Choose to accept God's gift of salvation today before it's too late.

The promise of eternal life is what will motivate you to live a life of purpose, guided by love, compassion, and helping others. We should always strive to be more like God in our daily lives. I remember many years ago, there was a bracelet going around with WWJD on it. In fact, there were many objects with this phrase on it, but I only had the bracelet. "What would Jesus Do" on any kind of wearable merchandise was the going thing back in my teenage years. I don't know if I wore it because it was pretty or if I wore it because of the message on it, but it's a message we all need to think about. No matter where we go or what we do, we should all be thinking about whether our actions are honorable to God. If people were thinking more about Jesus, maybe this world would be a better place instead of rampant with fighting and cruelty.

God's promise of eternal life provides us with hope, comfort, and a reason to obtain a deeper relationship with God. It shapes our worldview, influences our choices, and impacts how we interact with others. When you realize all God has done for you, you will be so appreciative and want to do more for this world and the people in it. It made me want to read my Bible even more when I realized how much God was blessing me through the little things in life. God wanting us to be with him in Heaven forever is even more reason to study His word. "Create in me a clean heart, O God; and renew a right spirit within me. Cast me not away from thy presence; and take not thy Holy Spirit from me. Restore unto me the joy of thy salvation; and withhold me with thy free spirit" (Psalms 51:10-12).

I still remember the day that I accepted Jesus in my heart. It was so amazing, and my heart was made brand new. I felt the Holy Spirit inside my heart, where He will be for all eternity. I hope you know Jesus and have the Holy Spirit in your heart. If not, then don't delay because you don't want to wait until it's too late. Remember, you never know when your last moment on this earth will be; only God knows.

Eternal life can be both a blessing and a curse because if you have Jesus in your heart and know you're going to Heaven, then you look forward to eternal life with God; however, if you haven't accepted the free gift of salvation before you die, then you will end up in the darkness of Hell for eternity. I don't like to talk about the bad things, but we should all be prepared for where we will end up. Even now, while you're on this earth, you prepare to have enough money to pay bills and go on vacation money. So why don't you prepare for the afterlife and make sure you go to Heaven? God loves you and wants the best for you and your life; however, He won't force you to accept Him and His free gift of salvation. He wants you to make that choice.

The promise of eternal life is tied to the idea of a new creation. Eternal life symbolizes a new life being created, and in many ways, that happens. You are born again when you accept the gift of eternal life because your old ways are forgiven and washed away, and you get to start over. Any sin that you commit will start at the point of your new life since accepting Jesus. You won't need to repent for past sins because they have already been forgiven and thrown away.

Eternal life begins in your life now. The moment you accept Jesus into your heart and the gift of eternal life, your eternal life will begin. "For God so loved the world, that he gave His only begotten Son, that whosoever believeth in Him should not perish, but have everlasting life" (John 3:16). Through your relationship with God, you will experience spiritual renewal, transformation, and a taste of the joy and peace that you will see in Heaven in the afterlife.

Eternal life in Heaven comes with rewards for faithful service and perseverance, but you will most likely want to give them back to God for all He has done for you. This promise of eternal life will also involve a transformation of your character, where you are sanctified and conformed into the likeness of Christ, growing in love, righteousness, and holiness.

We are all born with a sinful nature due to the fall of Adam and Eve. This sin separates us from God and leads to spiritual death. The promise of eternal life is available through the salvation and redemption created through Jesus Christ's sacrificial death and resurrection. By accepting Jesus as Savior of your life, your sins are forgiven, and you are reconciled with God, gaining access to the promise of eternal life. The belief in eternal life creates Heavenly hope that transcends earthly concerns. Even when this world is a bit crazy, we can set our minds on Heavenly things and look forward to the day we will be with our Lord and Savior. When you're thinking about Heaven, the worries of this world don't seem to matter.

This book is full of promises of God. There are many more I could have written about, but these seem to be the most important in my life. The most important promise is the promise of eternal life, and we all need to make sure we have that promise in our lives.

I've used several of my life experiences to show you how God is truly my life and how He has taken care of me and blessed me throughout my life. I know He's not through yet. I truly hope these promises of God have encouraged and blessed your heart. Now you need to let others know about the promises of God you just read and learned about. Spread the good news about God and His gift of eternal life so that everyone can experience hope and joy in their lives, too.

Printed in the USA
CPSIA information can be obtained
at www.ICGtesting.com
LVHW022138260124
770065LV00046B/1514